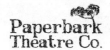 

Presented by Paperbark Theatre Company
in association with Thinking Aloud and Theatre503

THE DARK ROOM

BY ANGELA BETZIEN

The Dark Room had its UK premiere at Theatre503, London,
on 8 November 2017

The Dark Room won Best New Australian Work
at the 2011 Sydney Theatre Awards, following a production at the
Belvoir Street Downstairs Theatre in Sydney

THE DARK ROOM

BY ANGELA BETZIEN

CAST

Grace	Annabel Smith
Anni	Katy Brittain
Stephen	Tamlyn Henderson
Emma	Fiona Skinner
Craig	Alasdair Craig
Joseph	Paul Adeyefa

CREATIVE TEAM

Director	Audrey Sheffield
Designer	Jemima Robinson
Lighting Designer	Will Monks
Sound Designer	Jon McLeod
Movement Director	Annie-Lunnette Deakin-Foster
Casting Consultant	Marc Frankum
Assistant Director	Lilac Yosiphon

PRODUCTION TEAM

Producer	Paperbark Theatre
Associate Producer	Thinking Aloud
Stage Manager	Tomos Derrick
Production Manager	Kimberley Wyn Jones
PR	Chloe Nelkin Consulting

CAST

ANNABEL SMITH – GRACE
Annabel trained at The Oxford School of Drama.

Theatre includes: *The Last Ones* (Jermyn Street Theatre); *Flask, Manifesto, The Lighthouse* (The Space Theatre; named The Space's 'Performer of the year 2016'); *The Ajax Project* (Camden People's Theatre).

Theatre whilst in training: *Black Sheep* (Soho Theatre); *Anna Karenina* (Pegasus Theatre/Royal Court).

Radio includes: *Road to Oxford* (BBC Radio 4).

KATY BRITTAIN – ANNI
Katy trained at Webber Douglas Academy of Dramatic Art.

Theatre includes: *The Deep Blue Sea, Ugly Lies the Bone, Children's Hour* (National Theatre); *Les Liaisons Dangereuses, A Midsummer Night's Dream* (RSC); *Handbagged, Cat on a Hot Tin Roof* (West End); *Hamlet, Peter Pan, A Midsummer Night's Dream* (Crucible, Sheffield); *Noises Off, Rookery Nook, A Little Hotel On The Side, Private Lives* (Royal Lyceum Edinburgh).

TV includes: *The Bill, Midsomer Murders, Foyle's War*.

Film includes: *Indian Summer*.

TAMLYN HENDERSON – STEPHEN
Tamlyn trained at the West Australian Academy of Performing Arts.

UK theatre includes: *The Wind in the Willows* (Kew Gardens); *The Gruffalo* (Tall Stories); *A Porthole into the Minds of the Vanquished* (Guilded Balloon/Soho Theatre); *The Jinglists* (Underbelly/Soho Theatre).

Australian theatre includes: *Ladies in Black* (Queensland Theatre Company); *Les Miserables* (Cameron Mackintosh); *Sound of Music* (GFO); *The Importance of Being Earnest* (Seymour Centre); *How to Act Around Cops, Falsettos* (Darlinghurst Theatre Company); *Calamity Jane* (Neglected Musicals); *We Will Rock You* (Japan tour); *Cabaret* (IMG); *Circumspecto* (Sydney Opera House); *A Porthole into the Minds of the Vanquished* (Sydney Opera House/Malthouse Theatre)

TV includes: *All Saints, Redfern Now, As Actors-Manila* (web series).

Film includes: *Careless Love, Cedar Boys*.

FIONA SKINNER – EMMA
Since graduating from drama school Fiona has worked on an eclectic mix of projects.

These include: *Taboo* (4 episodes), *A Royal Night Out, Holby City, Birds of a Feather* (3 episodes), *Call the Midwife, Our Girl, NSFW, Doctors* (4 episodes), *Oakwood* and *Little Big House*.

She recently finished playing Jean in the No.1 Tour of *The Full Monty*.

She also appeared in the world premiere of Timberlake Wertenbaker's stage play, *Our Ajax*, was a member of the 2012 Old Vic New Voices Company and workshopped the new plays *Heroine*, *Apophis*, *My Imaginary Friend Patrick Stewart* and *People Like Us*.

Fiona was nominated for the Spotlight Prize in 2009.

ALASDAIR CRAIG – CRAIG

Alasdair trained at Webber Douglas Academy of Dramatic Art.

Theatre includes: *War Horse* (National Theatre/West End); *Not About Heroes* (tour/Trafalgar Studios); *A Midsummer Night's Dream*, *The Comedy of Errors*, *Pocket Dream*, *Twelfth Night*, *The Taming Of The Shrew*, *The Winter's Tale* (Propellor Theatre Company; UK/world tours, West End/New York); *A Few Man Fridays* (Riverside Studios); *She Rode Horses Like The Stock Exchange* (Old Vic, New Voices); *Arcadia* (Library Theatre, The Lowry); *All My Sons* (Curve, Leicester); *Major Barbara* (National Theatre); *Don Quixote* (West Yorkshire Playhouse/Madrid); *Black Comedy* (Colorado Festival of World Theatre); *The Quick* (Tristan Bates Theatre); *The Madness Of George Dubya* (New Players' Theatre); *The Rivals* (Ustinov, Bath).

Film and television includes: *EastEnders*, *The Royal*, *Doctors*, *POV*, *Lawless Heart*.

PAUL ADEYEFA – JOSEPH

Theatre includes: *Play of Thrones* (Union Theatre); *Result* (Pleasance Theatre); *The Window/Blank Pages* (Hope Theatre).

Television includes: *Cucumber* (Channel 4); *DCI Banks* (ITV) and *Ransom* (CBS).

Film includes: *Chubby Funny*.

CREATIVE TEAM

ANGELA BETZIEN – WRITER
Angela Betzien is an award-winning playwright and screenwriter.

Her work includes *Dog Wins Lotto* (Queensland Theatre Company, 1997); *Playboy of the Working Class* (Queensland Theatre Company, 2001); *Princess of Suburbia* (Real TV, 2001); *Kingswood Kids* (La Boite Theatre, 2002); *The Orphanage Project* (Queensland Theatre Company, 2003); *Children of the Black Skirt* (Queensland Arts Council and Real TV, 2003); *Hoods* (Sydney Opera House:Ed and Regional Arts Victoria, 2006); *Girl Who Cried Wolf* (Arena Theatre, 2008 & Windmill Theatre, 2011); *The Dark Room* (Black Swan Theatre Company, 2009; Belvoir, 2011); *The Teenage Alchemist* (Camp Quality, 2009) and *War Crimes* (Real TV, 2011).

Children of the Black Skirt, *Hoods* and *War Crimes* have been published by Currency Press.

Angela had two world-premiere play productions in 2016: *The Hanging* at Sydney Theatre Company and *Egg* at Melbourne Theatre Company. *The Hanging* was shortlisted for the NSW Premier Literary Awards 2017. *Helicopter* (originally MTC commissioned and produced) had its second season at the Norwegian National Theatre in Oslo, where it played in repertory in 2015 and 2016.

Angela was the Patrick White Fellow at Sydney Theatre Company in 2013, a recipient of the 2015 Australian Writers' Foundation Playwriting Award, and she won an AWGIE in 2015 for Community and Youth Theatre for co-writing *The Gap*. In 2016, Real TV was awarded Brilliant Careers funding by Screen Australia to accelerate Angela's transition to film and television writing.

AUDREY SHEFFIELD – DIRECTOR
Audrey Sheffield, founder and Artistic Director of Thinking Aloud, is a freelance theatre director.

Recent directing credits include: *We Too Are Giants* (Tricycle Theatre); *The Scar Test* (Theatre Delicatessen, Sheffield, Arcola, Colchester and Bedford); *Oresteia: A Response* (Almeida Theatre); *Little Flower of East Orange* (National Theatre Studio); *Almost Near* (Finborough Theatre); *June* (Park Theatre); *Bohemians* (Etcetera Theatre); *Moony's Kid Don't Cry* (King's Head Theatre).

As Associate/Assistant Director: *Don Juan in Soho* – dir. Patrick Marber, *Dead Funny* – dir. Terry Johnson, *Hand To God* – dir. Moritz von Stuelpnagel, *One Man, Two Guvnors* – dir. Nicholas Hytner (West End); *Electra* – dir. Ian Rickson (Old Vic); *Rapture, Blister, Burn* – dir. Peter DuBois, *Lay Down Your Cross* – dir. Clare Lizzimore (Hampstead Theatre); *The Effect* – dir. Rupert Goold (National Theatre); *Antony & Cleopatra* – dir. Tarell Alvin McCraney (RSC).

JEMIMA ROBINSON – DESIGNER
Jemima is the current recipient of the Max Rayne Design Bursary at the National Theatre. Jemima is the winner of the biennial Linbury Prize for Stage Design and the Bristol Old

Vic Technical Theatre Award in 2011. She is a former resident artist at Kenya's Kuona Arts Trust in Nairobi and resident designer for Istanbul's Talimhane Theatre.

Her recent UK design credits include: *The Majority* (National Theatre); *New Nigerians*, *Thebes Land* (nominated for Best Set Design and winner of Best Production: Offie Awards), *Maria de Buenos Aires* (Arcola Theatre); *Parallel Yerma* (Young Vic); *License to Ill*, *This Will End Badly* (Southwark Playhouse); *Biedermann and the Arsonists* (Sadler's Wells); *Mapping Brent* (Tricycle Theatre); *Dyl*, *Sparks* (Old Red Lion Theatre); *Hearing Things* (Albany Theatre).

WILL MONKS – LIGHTING DESIGNER
Will trained at Bristol Old Vic Theatre School.

Theatre includes: *Who Cares, Dust, Bare Skin on Briny Waters, PreScribed, E15, I Am Joan, Tanya, Shaedates: Or How I Learned to Love Myself* (UK tours); *We Live By the Sea* (nominated for Best Ensemble and Best Production, Offie Awards); *This Is Where We Live* (international tours); *When We Ran* (Pleasance Edinburgh); *Dyl* (Old Red Lion Theatre); *The Benidorm Elvis Fiesta* (Benidorm Palace); *Chilcot* (The Lowry, Battersea Arts Centre); *Dangerous or Otherwise, How to Survive the Blitz and Other Things, Time Passes. Listen.* (site specific); *Fuse* (Sheffield Theatres); *The Secret Slowness of Movement* (David Roberts Art Foundation).

JON MCLEOD – SOUND DESIGNER
Jon studied Sound Design (BA) at Leeds College of Music and Advanced Theatre Practice (MA) at Central School of Speech and Drama.

Recent credits include: *Spine, Tribute Acts, Ross & Rachel, Lost in the Neuron Forest, A Conversation, The Fanny Hill Project, Penguinpig, Tell Me Anything* (UK tour); *Food, Just To Get Married, I'm Gonna Pray For You So Hard* (Finborough Theatre); *If We Got Some More Cocaine I Could Show You How I Love You* (Old Red Lion Theatre); *Heartbreak Hotel* (The Jetty); *Macbeth, Followers* (Southwark Playhouse); *Arthur's World, The Rest Of Your Life* (Bush Theatre); *Screens* (Theatre503); *Free Fall* (Pleasance); *Stink Foot* (The Yard); *The Boy in Darkness, Nightmare Dreamer, Flying Roast Goose* (Blue Elephant Theatre); *Fair Field, Party Skills for the End of the World, 66 Minutes in Damascus* (Shoreditch Town Hall); *Strangers In Between* (King's Head Theatre); *Borderline Vultures* (The Lowry); *Organs of Little Apparent Importance* (HighTide Festival).

LILAC YOSIPHON – ASSISTANT DIRECTOR
Lilac Yosiphon trained at Mountview Academy of the Arts.

She is a theatre director, writer and the artistic director of Althea Theatre. She previously directed *The Freedom of the City* (Cockpit Theatre); *Salt* (Karamel Club); *Pablo* (Greenwich Theatre); *untranslatable.* (The Space Theatre); *You Tweet My Face Space* (Edinburgh Fringe) and *One Last Thing (For Now)* (Old Red Lion); which was nominated for an Off-West End Award for Best Ensemble. She was the associate director on *Dyl* (Old Red Lion Theatre); *The Playboy of The Western World* (Southwark Playhouse); and assistant director on *Dry Land* (Jermyn Street Theatre) and *Armstrong's War* (Finborough Theatre). She's currently endorsed by Arts Council England as a promising Exceptional Talent in the UK.

TOMOS DERRICK – STAGE MANAGER

Tomos studied at Stage Management and Technical Theatre at LAMDA.

Recent stage management credits include: *Hyem* (Theatre503).

KIMBERLEY WYN JONES – PRODUCTION MANAGER

Kimberley trained at Bristol Old Vic Theatre School graduating this July.

Credits whilst training: Production Manager on *13* (Tobacco Factory Bristol); *Sex With a Stranger, Iceland, I Am the Wind* and *Crave* (Wardrobe Theatre Bristol); and a tour of *Jason and the Argonauts*. Assistant Production Manager on *Julius Caesar* (Bristol Old Vic); *Our Town* (Circomedia); *Two Gentlemen of Verona, Treasure Island* and *Our Country's Good* (Redgrave Theatre Bristol); and a tour of *Whilst Shepherds Watched*.

Kimberley recently worked on a two-month placement with the production management team on *Angels in America* at the National Theatre.

Kimberley made her professional Production Management debut this summer with *The Love of the Nightingale* at Circomedia in Bristol, and is thrilled to be working on *The Dark Room*.

ANNIE-LUNNETTE DEAKIN-FOSTER – MOVEMENT DIRECTOR

Annie-Lunnette is a contemporary dance theatre choreographer, maker and movement director who is also a co-founding member of the award winning company, C-12 Dance Theatre. She trained at Middlesex University.

Movement Director/choreography credits include: *Trump's Women* (RADA); *The Little Match Girl and Other Happier Tales* (Shakespeare's Globe); *i know all the secrets of my world* (Latitude Festival/Watford Palace Theatre/The Porter Theatre/Pegasus Theatre Oxford/Salisbury Playhouse/Unity Theatre/Lincoln Drill Hall/Bristol Old Vic/The Lowry/The Drum/Nottingham Playhouse/Mercury Theatre/The Albany).

Dance credits include: *Shhh!* (Dance City/MAC Birmingham/New Wolsey Ipswich/Norwich Playhouse/The Woodville Gravesend/CircoMedia Bristol/Winchester Theatre Royal); *The Van Man* (Watch This Space at the National Theatre/St Albans Festival/Freedom Festival Hull/The Albany Outdoors).

SHAELEE ROOKE – PRODUCER

Shaelee is the producer for Paperbark Theatre Company, and previous Resident Assistant Producer at Theatre503.

Producing credits include: *This is Where We Live* (Alma Theatre, Bristol; Assembly, Edinburgh Fringe; Sheen Centre, New York International Fringe Festival; SoHo Playhouse, New York City); and *Shaedates: or how I learned to love myself* (Edinburgh Fringe Festival/regional tour).

Shaelee is the Co-Producer for comedy trio Darcy, Rooke & Hinds and Sharp Teeth (The London Edition). She is also the Assistant Producer for the Sleeping Trees.

Shaelee trained as an actor at the Bristol Old Vic Theatre School and starred in Paperbark's award-winning debut production of *This is Where We Live* alongside Oliver de Rohan.

PRESENTED BY PAPERBARK THEATRE IN ASSOCIATION WITH THINKING ALOUD AND THEATRE503

PAPERBARK THEATRE

Paperbark was founded in 2013 by Oliver de Rohan and Shaelee Rooke, graduates of the Bristol Old Vic Theatre School, with the aim of championing new Australian plays to international audiences.

Paperbark's debut production of Vivienne Walshe's *This is Where We Live* toured to international fringe festivals, and received critical acclaim (Five Stars & Critics' Pick, Time Out New York). Following a sell-out season at the New York International Fringe Festival, it won the Excellence Award for Best Overall Play and was selected to appear in the Fringe Encore Series at the SoHo Playhouse; a selection of the best work from the Edinburgh and New York International Fringe Festivals.

THINKING ALOUD

Thinking Aloud is a new theatre company, founded by Audrey Sheffield, dedicated to making honest, bold and ambitious new work. *The Dark Room* will be their debut production.

OUR SUPPORTERS

We would like to thank all of the generous individuals who kindly donated to our crowdfunding campaign.

Thank you to Lenny Adam, Caitlin Albery Beavan, Yasmeen Arden, Simon Bailey, Peter Baker, Stephen & Ali Barran, Gabrielle Bobrovizki, Elizabeth Bowe, Rebecca Bridle, Jessica Campbell, Claire Clements, Simon Coates, Freya Crawshaw, Adrian Davies, Maria and Bryan David, Dan Davies, Beverley Eve, the de Moraville family, Patrick Fleming, Emma Fielding, James Foster, Carl Fullilove, Rupert Goold, Lesley Higgs, Emma Hinds, Lily Hirsch, Jackie Hooper, Julia Ingram, Monica Jankel, Hannah Khalil, Andy Kelly, Debbie Korley, Rob Kraitt, Artem Kreimer, Rob Laird, Max Lindsay, Richard Lodge, James Manning, Patrick Marber, Rose Marter, Alison McLean, Tarell McCraney, Gerri McKenna, Missmanaged Theatre Company, Dominique Moore, Andrea Morris, Siân Mulligan, Brian Mullin, Daniel Multer, Emma Naomi, Ricardo Navas, Nye Pascoe & Amy Reitsma, Victoria Penn, Sue Prebble, Rashida Punja, Emma Reynolds, Tim Roseman, Drew Rooke, Suzie Rooke & Ramesh Karwal, Arinder Sadhra, Sally, Archie Sample, Laura Sedgwick, Ian Shiner, Paul Sockett, Laura & Phil Sutton, The Sun Apparatus Theatre Company, Anna & John Tolputt, Louise Torres-Ryan, Tom Van Avermaet, Jonathan Wakeham, Ross & Lynne Warner, Alex Welsh, Pauline Wickham and Thomas Yarrow.

Special thanks to the late Rod Nicholls, Nica Burns, Ann David, David & Sophie Shalit, Jonathan & Jacqueline Gestetner, Julian Dawes & Ann Rau Dawes, Michael David, Jennifer Mushumani, Bruce Gordon, Matthew Nelson, Jessica Campbell, Michael Ogden and Trish Wadley.

We would also like to thank F H Space for their lovely rehearsal space, the Young Vic Costume Department, Matt Cooper for his brilliant photography, Theatre503 for their endless support, Sharky & George, the Directors Charitable Foundation, the Agent General for South Australia, the Menzies Centre for Australian Studies, Peter Lehmann Wines and our official charity partner, the NSPCC (Registered charity numbers 216401 and SC037717).

THEATRE 503

Theatre503 is an award-winning theatre which supports and stages more first-time writers than any other theatre in the country. At the heart of this commitment is a belief that the most important element in a writer's development is to see their work on a stage, in front of an audience, performed to the highest professional standard. Over 100 new pieces of work are staged at 503 in a year, ranging from 1-2 night short pieces to full length 4-week runs. Careers started at 503 include Tom Morton-Smith (*Oppenheimer*), Anna Jordan (*Yen*), Katori Hall (*The Mountaintop*) and Jon Brittain (*Rotterdam*) – the last two productions started at 503 and won Olivier Awards.

Theatre503 Team

Artistic Director	Lisa Spirling
Executive Director	Andrew Shepherd
Producer	Jake Orr
Literary Manager	Steve Harper
Operations Manager	Anna De Freitas
Marketing Coordinator	Rebecca Usher
Technical Manager	Alastair Borland
Literary Associate	Lauretta Barrow
Literary Coordinator	Wayne Brown
Resident Assistant Producers	Helen Milne, Samara Thomas
Interns	Holly Dixon, Taylor Dahlberg

Theatre503 Board

Erica Whyman (Chair)
Royce Bell (Vice Chair)
Chris Campbell
Kay Ellen Consolver
Joachim Fleury
Celine Gagnon
Eleanor Lloyd
Marcus Markou
Geraldine Sharpe-Newton
Jack Tilbury
Roy Williams OBE

Theatre503 Volunteers

Aydan Tair, Laura Sedgwick, Rob Ellis, Nathalie Czarnecki, Asha Osborne, Emma Griffiths, Carla Kingham, Tom Hartwell, Kelly Agredo, Ceri Lothian, Annabel Pemberton, Uju Enendu, George Linfield, Kay Benson, Angelique MacDonald, Ciaran Chillingworth, Amelia Madan, Christina Murdock, Eve Richards, Faaiz Mbelizi, Sussan Sanii, Berit Moback, Dominica Kedzierska, Lucy Robson, Gareth Jones, Emma Anderson, Yasmine Dankwah, Abbiegale Duncanson, Paul Sockett, Sian Thomas, Kai Johnson, Mara Vodinelic, Rachel Tookey, Olivia Munk.

THEATRE503 SUPPORTERS

Theatre503's work would not be possible without the support of the following individuals, trusts and organisations:

Current Patrons: Angela Hyde-Courtney, Cas & Philip Donald, Darryl Eales, David Baxter, Erica Whyman, Flow Associates, Geraldine Sharpe-Newton, Jill Segal, Kay Ellen Consolver, Marcus Markou, Michael North, Mike Morfey, Pam Alexander and Rotha Bell.

Arts Council England Grants for the Arts, The Boris Karloff Foundation, The Peter Wolff Trust, The Schroder Charity Trust, The Sylvia Waddilove Foundation, Unity Theatre Trust, Wandsworth Borough Council.

Nick Hern Books, The Harold Hyam Wingate Foundation, Curtis Brown and Ben Hall for their support of the Playwriting Award.

The Orseis Trust for their support of the 503Five.

M&G Investments and Barbara Broccoli for their support of our Five-O-Fresh Young Creative Leaders Project.

Jack Tilbury, Plann, Dynamics, CharcoalBlue, Stage Solutions, Bush Theatre & Will Bowen for their support in refurbishing our seats.

Theatre503 is in receipt of funding from Arts Council England's Catalyst: Evolve fund, match funding every pound raised in new income until July 2019.

We are particularly grateful to Philip and Christine Carne and the long-term support of the Richard Carne Trust for our Playwriting Award and 503Five.

THE DARK ROOM

Angela Betzien

For Charmaine

Foreword
Angela Betzien

Several years ago I was working on an education project in regional Queensland. The principal of the small primary school talked to me at length about the severe shortage of accommodation for young people at risk. These children are often supervised by youth workers, in what is termed 'commercial accommodation'. This occurs until a placement in a foster home or residential facility becomes available. Often this takes several days, weeks or even months. Generally the children who are 'homed' in motels are those that are the most difficult to accommodate elsewhere; the kids with severe psychological and behavioral problems, the ones who require and deserve the greatest care and attention. This disturbing reality formed one of the starting points for this play.

In Australia we have a long and dark history of neglecting, abusing and forgetting the most vulnerable in our communities, our children. Justice will only come when we as a society acknowledge what the dead have suffered and what the living continue to endure, when we cease repeating the mistakes of the past, when we take action to truly protect all children, not just our own.

Background

In April 1991, a Royal Commission into Aboriginal deaths in custody was released. The chief Commissioner Eliot Johnson wrote, 'I had no conception of the degree... of abuse of personal power, utter paternalism, open contempt and total indifference with which so many Aboriginal people were visited on a daily basis.' Of the 339 recommendations made by the Royal Commission, none called for criminal charges. Several of the key recommendations have not been properly implemented in many states. Despite the inquiry, Aboriginal deaths in custody continue to occur at an alarming and unacceptable rate.

On June 21st 2007, the federal government announced the intervention in the Northern Territory. This 'national emergency' was initiated in response to the release of the *Little Children Are Sacred* report by Pat Anderson and Rex Wild. This report was an inquiry into the abuse and neglect of Aboriginal children in the Northern Territory. In their report they state, 'What is required is a determined, coordinated effort to break the cycle and provide the necessary strength, power and appropriate support and services to local communities, so they can lead themselves out of the malaise: in a word, *empowerment*!' Many of the measures undertaken as part of the Intervention have no link at all to the issue of child abuse. The suspension of the Racial Discrimination Act, mandatory 'income management' and government acquisition of indigenous controlled land, have been widely condemned, nationally and internationally, as racist, and disempowering. Anderson and Wild have both publicly expressed concern over the Government's use of the report to justify the Intervention. The Intervention continues today.

Acknowledgements

Adam Mitchell and the 2009 HotBed Ensemble, Lee Lewis, Brendan Cowell and the Sydney Theatre Company Push Program, Carly Leonard and Carolina Walkington from HLA Management, Jodie Le Vesconte, Ralph Myers, Anthea Williams and Belvoir, Jean Mostyn and The Yellow Agency, Leticia Caceres, Pete Goodwin, Leah Purcell, Bjorn Stewart, Cameron Stewart, Billie Rose Prichard, Anna Lise Phillips, Michael Hankin, Christopher Page, Jada Alberts, Brianna Pike, Heidrun Lohr.

The Dark Room was first performed at the Perth Institute of Contemporary Arts (PICA) on 1 March 2009, with the following cast:

Arielle Gray
Natalie Holmwood
Jacinta John
Will O'Mahony
Tom O'Sullivan
Kazimir Sas

Director	Adam Mitchell
Set and Costume Designer	Alicia Clements
Lighting Designer	Trent Suidgeest
Sound Designer	Ben Collins

The Dark Room was revived at Belvoir St Theatre, Sydney, on 3 November 2011, with the following cast:

Brendan Cowell
Anna Lise Phillips
Billie Rose Prichard
Leah Purcell
Bjorn Stewart
Cameron Stewart

Director	Leticia Cáceres
Designer	Michael Hankin
Lighting Designer	Christopher Page
Composer and Sound Designer	Pete Goodwin (The Sweats)

Characters

ANNI, *early forties*
GRACE, *fourteen*
STEPHEN, *mid-thirties*
EMMA, *mid-thirties*
CRAIG, *late forties*
JOSEPH, *nineteen*

The action takes place in the same room with characters moving in and out of focus and time.

A three-star motel room in the Northern Territory.

ANNI *enters with a key.*

She is carrying a single sunflower.

She switches on a lamp and goes to the bathroom.

GRACE *appears at the door. She is wearing a dirty pillowcase over her head, small eyes cut out. A dog-like face is drawn on the pillowcase and the corners are twisted into ears.*

ANNI *emerges from the bathroom.*

ANNI   Come on.
                    It's all right.
                    Come on.
                    That's it.

                    GRACE *slowly edges inside the motel room.*

                    There you go.

                    ANNI *closes the door behind her.*

                    You're safe now it's safe here.

                    ANNI *nurses her hand.*

                    GRACE *stays at the door.*
                    ANNI *looks at her hand, it is raw and red.*

                    Going in there to wash this okay?

                    ANNI *heads into the bathroom. ANNI washes her hand under the tap.*

                    GRACE *removes a knife from her bag and hides it beneath the mattress.*

                    ANNI *peers out at GRACE.*

                    Still there?

                    ANNI *returns to the bathroom.*

Put your bag down Grace.
Make yourself comfortable.

Pause.

You remember me don't you?
You know who I am.

ANNI *emerges from the bathroom, nursing her hand.*

Picked you up from school once remember?
We went to the wildlife park.

Pause.

You've seen where I work.
Been there a few times haven't you?

Silence.

Are you hungry?

ANNI *takes a McDonald's bag from her bag.*

This is for you.
Thirsty?

Silence.

You're safe Grace
This is a safe place.

Silence.

Are you hot?
I'm hot.
Hot in here don't you think?

Silence.

Why don't you put your bag down?
Put it down here on the bed hey.

GRACE *clings to her backpack.*

You remember me don't you?
You gunna show me your face?

Silence.

ANNI's *mobile rings.*

ANNI *checks the phone but doesn't answer.*

GRACE	Someone in here.
ANNI	Just you and me.
GRACE	Someone else.
ANNI	There isn't have a look.
GRACE	What's this place?
ANNI	It's a motel.
GRACE	Not stayin' here.
ANNI	It's just for tonight. I'll find somewhere else for you in the morning.
GRACE	What's happening to me?
ANNI	You've been taken into care. You called me didn't you? You said Grace is in trouble.
GRACE	Who called you?
ANNI	You did Grace.
GRACE	What took you so long?
ANNI	I came as fast as I could. It's a long drive out of town. Couldn't find you.

Pause.

What were you doing under the house?
Hey?
Who were you hiding from?

GRACE *is silent.*

You bit me.

GRACE	No.

ANNI   You did Grace.
                Who'd you think I was?

                GRACE *doesn't respond*.

                Was your mum out there?
                Thought I saw her.

                Pause.

                I drove you here.
                You slept in the car.

GRACE   Someone in here.

ANNI   Just you and me.
                Two's company hey.
                Why don't you put your bag down?

                Silence.

                Do you wanna shower?
                There are towels in there.
                Do you wanna sleep?
                Do you wanna watch TV?
                Let's see if there's a movie.
                Where's the remote?

                ANNI *finds the remote control near the
                television. She offers it to* GRACE. GRACE
                turns away.

                Okay what do you want to do?

GRACE   Want you to leave.
                Want you to leave me alone.

ANNI   Yeah well can't do that.

GRACE   Yes.

ANNI   Nuh.

GRACE   Can.

ANNI   I have to stay with you.

GRACE   Want to be by myself.

ANNI	Not going to happen.
GRACE	Yes.
ANNI	Yeah when that desert out there freezes over.
GRACE	Have to go in there.
ANNI	I'll stand outside the door.
GRACE	Perve on me?
ANNI	No thanks.
GRACE	You're a paedophile.
ANNI	Yeah that's me.
GRACE	What am I gunna do?

ANNI   I won't look.
You can trust me.
Go on
hurry up.

GRACE   Don't want to now.

Pause.

ANNI   You play cards?
I got a deck in the glove box.
No?
What about we get some mags from the servo
real trashy ones?
Get all the goss on the stars.
Hey who's your favourite celebrity Grace?
Me I like that Angelina Jolie.
Reckon she's great.

GRACE *is silent.*

What do you wanna do then?

GRACE   Masturbate.
Feel much better if I have a wank.
So you go in there and shut the door okay?

ANNI   Not okay no.

GRACE	You wanna watch?
	GRACE *puts her hand down her pants*.
	I'm wet.
	GRACE *licks her fingers*.
ANNI	Can't do that Grace.
GRACE	You're boring got a pole up your arse.
	GRACE *darts to the bathroom*.
ANNI	Leave the door open.
GRACE	Paedo.
	ANNI *searches the room for dangerous objects*.
ANNI	Grace?
	She hides the objects in her bag.
	Grace?
	GRACE *emerges from the bathroom*.
GRACE	I'm bleeding.
ANNI	Where are you bleeding? Have you cut yourself?
GRACE	From my cunt. Got my period. My first time. I lie.
ANNI	We'll go to the servo get you something.
	ANNI *rummages through her own bag*.
GRACE	I'll stay here.
ANNI	We've been through this.
GRACE	Got pains.
ANNI	You have to come with me.
GRACE	Just stuff toilet paper up my gash.

ANNI   Wait up.

                ANNI *finds a sanitary pad in her bag and hands it to* GRACE.

                Here you go.

                GRACE *peels it and sticks it on the pillow.*

GRACE   Have you put away all the sharp things?

ANNI   You can take that off now.
                Make it yourself?
                Is it a dog?
                Do you like dogs?
                You've got a lot of dogs out home haven't you?

                GRACE *is silent.*

                What do you say Grace?
                Will you show me your face?

                Pause.

GRACE   Not stayin' here.

ANNI   Where else you going?

GRACE   Beach.

ANNI   Long way.
                How you getting there?

GRACE   Drive.

ANNI   You can drive can ya?

GRACE   Yep.

ANNI   Won't get far.

GRACE   I'm going.

ANNI   Think I'll let you?

GRACE   Wait till you fall asleep.

ANNI   I don't sleep.

GRACE   Gotta sleep.

ANNI	Not me.
GRACE	You're a zombie.
ANNI	Maybe.
GRACE	Not stayin' here.
ANNI	Have to.
GRACE	Can't tell me what to do.
ANNI	I'm responsible for you.
GRACE	No you're not.
ANNI	I am tonight.
GRACE	Then you'll dump me.
ANNI	I'll find you a placement.
GRACE	You can't find one.
ANNI	That's not true.
GRACE	Heard you on the phone.
ANNI	When?
GRACE	In the car.
ANNI	Thought you were asleep.
GRACE	Heard you leavin' messages beggin' 'em to take me.
ANNI	I will find somewhere.
GRACE	Where?

Pause.

| ANNI | I don't know yet. |
| GRACE | Not goin' to the res.
Got raped there.
Did.
That's your fault.
You took me. |

ANNI	I'll find somewhere. Somewhere you might like. Somewhere safe.
GRACE	Promise?
	Pause.
ANNI	I'll try Grace. I'll do the best I can.
GRACE	Not goin' to the Res again rather live on the street.
ANNI	Not much fun.
GRACE	No fun gettin' raped.
ANNI	What would you eat?
GRACE	McDonald's KFC whatever.
ANNI	How you going to pay for it?
GRACE	Steal it or busk I can sing.
ANNI	Oh yeah?
GRACE	Probably win *Australian Idol.*
ANNI	Go on then show me.
GRACE	Hey?
ANNI	Sing something.
GRACE	Sing for money not singin' for no reason.
ANNI	What do you reckon you're worth?
GRACE	Twenty bucks.
ANNI	Twenty? Must be pretty good.
	ANNI *finds a twenty in her wallet and places it on the bed.*
	Go on then.
GRACE	Givin' that to me?

ANNI	Yours if you sing You ever sung for anyone before?
GRACE	Yes.
ANNI	You wearing that on *Australian Idol*?
GRACE	No.
	GRACE *rips the pillowcase mask off.*
	She tries to sing but can't.
	Don't have to do anythin' I don't want.
ANNI	No.
GRACE	Don't.
ANNI	You don't that's true.
GRACE	Do somethin' else for that.
ANNI	Don't want anything else.
GRACE	Do it for ten.
ANNI	Said I don't want anything else.
	Pause.
GRACE	Don't you like me?
ANNI	Yes I like you Grace.
	Pause.
GRACE	You bought me an ice cream a Heart.
ANNI	When?
GRACE	At the park.
ANNI	So you remember that?
GRACE	We looked at the dingos.
ANNI	Yes.
GRACE	You had a green shirt on. Smoked Benson & Hedges. Had that round your neck.

Someone called.
Your face changed
your face went different.
You said I can't talk now I'm with a client.
You asked me questions.
Didn't answer 'em.
Poked a stick at the dingos.
You said that was cruel.
Then you bought me a Heart.

ANNI   At the kiosk that's right.

GRACE   Then I climbed on the wall.

            Pause.

ANNI   Yeah you did.

GRACE   I was going to jump.

ANNI   You were playing a game.

GRACE   I was going to.

ANNI   Were you?

GRACE   Didn't wanna go back.

ANNI   I know you didn't.

GRACE   You promised me.
            Said I didn't have to.
            You said I could live with you if I came
            down.

ANNI   No…

GRACE   You said.

ANNI   No Grace…

GRACE   You promised me.

ANNI   I was worried you'd fall.

GRACE   Crossed your heart and hoped to die.

ANNI   Could have hurt yourself.

GRACE   Then you broke it.

ANNI	It's my job to look after you.
GRACE	Made me go back anyway.
ANNI	Your family wanted you.

GRACE *shows* ANNI *a scar on her arm.*

GRACE	That night I cut this. It's a heart. It's forever. It's for you.
ANNI	I had to take you back Grace. Your mum wanted you. You know that.

Pause.

GRACE   There's a boy I know.
         He's a faggot.
         Wears dresses and that
         make-up.
         Wants to be a girl.
         Wants me to call him a she.
         He stays over at my place sometimes.
         I can make him do whatever I want.
         I put him on the chain under the house.
         Once I gave him dog food on toast and he ate
         it.
         I made him lick me.
         Did you hear that?
         I made him lick me.

ANNI	Oh yeah what's his name?
GRACE	No one.
ANNI	That kid from around here?
GRACE	Made it up.
ANNI	I know who you're talking about. Didn't know you were friends.
GRACE	Made it up I said.

GRACE *looks in the mirror.*

Think I look like a boy?
Cut my hair off with a razor.
Look like a pit bull.
Are you afraid of me?

ANNI	Nope.
GRACE	Why not?
ANNI	Cos I reckon your bark's worse than your bite.
GRACE	Do ya think I'm ugly?
ANNI	No.
GRACE	Yes you do.
ANNI	I think you're very pretty.
GRACE	Knew you were a paedo. I've booby-trapped this room.
ANNI	How've you done that?
GRACE	Not tellin' but if you try to rape me in the night an alarm'll go off and I'll wake up and stab ya.
ANNI	With what?
GRACE	Bite ya face off. Then you'll need a face transplant. Need one anyway you're ugly.
ANNI	You wanna know what's ugly?
GRACE	I am so are you.
ANNI	What's ugly is how you talk to people.
GRACE	That's my oppositional defiance disorder.
ANNI	I know what you're trying to do. I know this act. You're smarter than that.

GRACE	Nuh. I'm a retard.
ANNI	Can't bullshit me.

GRACE *grabs* ANNI's *bag, runs to the bathroom and locks the door.*

Open the door.
Open the door Grace.
Open it now.
Do you want me to call the hospital?
If you don't open the door I'm calling them.
You'll have to spend the night in the ward.
You know what that's like
I'm making the call.
I'm doing it now.

ANNI *picks up her mobile.*

GRACE *opens the door.*

GRACE *throws the bag on the bed.*

ANNI *searches the bag.*

Give them to me.
Give them to me.

GRACE	What?
ANNI	You know what.
GRACE	Ate them.
ANNI	Give them to me.
GRACE	Flushed them.
ANNI	Don't fuck me around.
GRACE	Oh you mean these?

GRACE *throws a prescription pill bottle across the bed.*

You sad Anni?

ANNI	Don't do that again.

GRACE	Sorry sorry Anni sorry Anni I'm sorry Anni Anni I'm sorry.
ANNI	Righto Grace.
GRACE	Sorry.
ANNI	Okay.
GRACE	Didn't call the hospital did you?
ANNI	No.
GRACE	Don't wanna go to the hospital.
ANNI	Then chill out Grace. Why don't we watch some TV? You choose here's the remote.

GRACE *grabs* ANNI*'s arm.*

GRACE	What's that?
ANNI	Scar. Twenty-three stitches.
GRACE	What from?
ANNI	Smashed it through a window. True.
GRACE	Hurt?
ANNI	Didn't feel a thing.

GRACE *kisses* ANNI *on the scar.*

GRACE *tries to kiss* ANNI *on the lips.*

ANNI *pushes* GRACE *away.*

No.
Can't do that.

GRACE	Let's go to your place. Yes. Let's get smashed.
ANNI	We're staying here tonight.
GRACE	Where do you live?

ANNI	In a flat.
GRACE	Who with?
ANNI	I live alone.
GRACE	Why?
ANNI	I choose to.
GRACE	Nobody loves you. What's that?
ANNI	What's what?
GRACE	That round your neck.
ANNI	This?
GRACE	Wearin' that at the park.
ANNI	Was I?
GRACE	It's special isn't it?
ANNI	Yes.
GRACE	It's a heart. It's a heart shape. Where'd you get it?
ANNI	Someone gave it to me.
GRACE	Who?
ANNI	A friend.
GRACE	Can I have it?
ANNI	No.
GRACE	Why not? Why not?
ANNI	Because it's mine.
GRACE	Never get what I want. Who was that on the phone?
ANNI	When?

GRACE	At the park you said I can't talk now I'm with a client. Who was that?

Pause.

ANNI	I don't remember.
GRACE	Your face changed. Your face went different.
ANNI	That was five years ago.
GRACE	Gunna be with you. Be with you like you promised. 'Member that promise you promised me Anni? Saying yes now saying yes to it saying yes please.
ANNI	I made a mistake Grace. I'm sorry. Made a promise I couldn't keep. Won't do that again. I'm sorry.

The phone rings.

GRACE	Don't answer it. Don't don't don't don't don't.
ANNI	Settle down Grace.

ANNI *checks the caller but doesn't answer.*

GRACE	You can't talk now you're with a client. You can't talk now you are with a client. You're with me now.
ANNI	I said settle down.
GRACE	Turn it off now.
ANNI	I'm not going to do that.
GRACE	Yes turn it off now.
ANNI	I need to leave it on.

GRACE	Yes turn it off.
ANNI	No Grace.
GRACE	Yes Grace we don't want to be disturbed. Put the sign on the door.

GRACE grabs the McDonald's bag and eats the burger like a ravenous dog.

The door of the motel room is opened.

STEPHEN sways at the door wearing a dishevelled, sweat-stained suit.

He is drunk.

EMMA pushes past STEPHEN. She rips off her shoes and stockings, drops her bag and collapses on the bed.

STEPHEN	Fuck it's hot. It's fucking hot in here.
EMMA	What's that smell?
STEPHEN	Is the air-con on?

EMMA absorbs the room.

EMMA	Couldn't you get somewhere else?
STEPHEN	Where's the remote?
EMMA	Somewhere in town.
STEPHEN	Can you see the remote?
EMMA	Somewhere nice.
STEPHEN	No.
EMMA	Why not?
STEPHEN	Wedding. Whole town's booked out for the big booze-up.
EMMA	Streets crawling with cops.

Pause.

	It's not safe out there.
STEPHEN	Safe as houses.
EMMA	Anything could happen.
STEPHEN	Who's gunna mess with us? We're cops.
EMMA	You're superheroes with superpowers.
STEPHEN	Didn't say that did I? Did I say that?
EMMA	Yeah well you were acting like a pack of dogs at the reception.
STEPHEN	It's been a fucked year.
EMMA	What was with all the dry-rooting on the dance floor?
STEPHEN	We were just mucking around letting off steam.
EMMA	Pissing on your territory more like.
STEPHEN	That reminds me gotta piss.

STEPHEN *goes to the bathroom*.

EMMA	Thank god it's over. I need a shower. Hey do you wanna have a shower with me?

STEPHEN *emerges from the bathroom*.

EMMA *enters the bathroom*.

STEPHEN	Listen Em…

Pause.

EMMA	What? What?
STEPHEN	The boys are pushing on they're pushing on to Dick's nightclub.

EMMA *is silent.*

There's a shuttle bus coming.
It's picking everyone up...

EMMA *is silent.*

I thought I'd go
just for a bit you know.
I should go.

EMMA	No.
STEPHEN	Em.
EMMA	No.
STEPHEN	Come on.
EMMA	You said you'd stay.
STEPHEN	It's been a fucked year.
EMMA	You're telling me.
STEPHEN	Don't be like this.
EMMA	You promised me.
STEPHEN	I don't want to.

Fuck I'd rather stay here with youse.
I'm just going for one or two.

Pause.

EMMA	Just one or two?
STEPHEN	Probably just the one.

A nightcap.
I'll catch a cab back.

EMMA	I'll come.
STEPHEN	What?
EMMA	I'll drive you.
STEPHEN	You said you were tired.
EMMA	For one drink

a nightcap.

STEPHEN   You'll just be bored.

EMMA   I'll be bored here look at this place.

STEPHEN   The bus is coming it's on its way.
You should relax put your feet up.

EMMA   Just give me a sec.

STEPHEN   We're heading to the club.

EMMA   Yeah I know.

STEPHEN   You won't be able to hear yourself think.
You know duff duff.
That's probably bad for the baby.
Its eyes and ears are being formed at the
moment you know.
I read that in your pregnancy book.
Probably happening as we speak.

STEPHEN speaks to the baby through
EMMA*'s stomach.*

Isn't that right kid?

STEPHEN *listens*.

Yeah he agrees with me.

EMMA   Don't be a dickhead.

STEPHEN   It's not like you can drink.

EMMA   I'd kill for a drink.

STEPHEN   Well you can't have one.

EMMA   Don't tell me.

STEPHEN   You have to be careful.

EMMA   I know that.

STEPHEN   We don't want a retard for a kid.

EMMA   Can you not use that word?

STEPHEN   What's wrong with retard?
It's a medical fucking term.

EMMA	Just don't.
STEPHEN	I see it all the time out here.
EMMA	All right for you. It's like it's not my body any more. Feel like I'm occupied or something.
STEPHEN	That's a really nice attitude for a mother-to-be. What do you want me to do? Suffer alongside you deny myself?
EMMA	Yeah.
STEPHEN	Give up the booze the smokes?
EMMA	Yeah that'd be nice.

Pause.

You can't can you?

STEPHEN	Piece of piss.
EMMA	Then do it.
STEPHEN	Done it. Six booze-free months. I'll get fit Detox join the gym boxercise.
EMMA	Would you?
STEPHEN	Yeah for you for the baby Course I would.

Pause.

Starting tomorrow.
Just let me get slaughtered.

Pause.

EMMA	I came back.

STEPHEN	I know.
EMMA	I came back from Sydney for you.
STEPHEN	I know that. Just give me tonight. All right? One more night then I'm done. I swear to you. All right?

EMMA *searches in her bag*.

You want me to make you a cuppa before
I go?
No?
Yes?
No?
Maybe?
Baby?

EMMA *ignores him*.

I'm off.
Em?
Em?

EMMA	What?
STEPHEN	I'll see you.
EMMA	When?
STEPHEN	In the morning.
EMMA	When in the morning?
STEPHEN	When you wake up.
EMMA	What if I can't sleep?
STEPHEN	Then you won't wake up.
EMMA	You'll be here?
STEPHEN	I'll be here in the morning.

We'll check out late go for brekkie.
Drive home early arvo.
Okay?

EMMA *is silent*.

Goodnight.
Goodnight.
I love you.
Hey baby girl.
I
Love
You.

STEPHEN *kisses* EMMA.

EMMA *bites* STEPHEN *on the lip*.

Fuck.
Why'd you do that?

STEPHEN *leaves*.

ANNI *is 'alone' in the room*.

ANNI *goes to the bathroom and emerges with the sunflower*.

STEPHEN *appears at the door and addresses* ANNI.

Thought it was you.

ANNI *returns the sunflower to the bathroom and faces* STEPHEN.

Saw your vehicle outside recognised the government number plates.
Stephen.
Constable Stephen Collins.

ANNI   Yeah I know who you are.

STEPHEN   You got a client staying here with you tonight?

Pause.

ANNI *nods*.

Kid here?

ANNI   No.

STEPHEN   Haven't arrived yet?

ANNI *shakes her head*.

Late isn't it?
Where they coming from?

ANNI *doesn't answer*.

STEPHEN *stares at her*.

Domestic?
Our boys call it in?

Pause.

ANNI   You got a cigarette?

STEPHEN *gives her a cigarette. He offers a
light but* ANNI *has pocketed the smoke for
later*.

STEPHEN   We get called out on DVOs four five nights a
week.
Fridays are shit
but Sundays are shockers.
Blokes on benders all weekend.
Same places every time you'd have to be
stupid.

Pause.

Wouldn't ya?
You know to hang around like a punching bag
waiting for the next...

STEPHEN *jabs the air*.

ANNI *steps back*.

STEPHEN *offers over a beer from his six-
pack*.

	You wanna drink?
ANNI	No.
STEPHEN	Go on.
ANNI	No thanks.
STEPHEN	Don't you drink?

ANNI *is silent*.

Fuck how do you manage that?
This is my medication.

Pause.

All these motels look exactly the same.
Can I use your bathroom?

| ANNI | No. |
| STEPHEN | I'm hanging for a piss
broke the seal. |

Pause.

Just be a sec.

ANNI	I'd rather you didn't.
STEPHEN	Just for a second.
ANNI	I'm waiting for a client. I don't want them to see you in here might frighten them.
STEPHEN	What?
ANNI	Cop sniffin' around you know.
STEPHEN	I'm not sniffin' around. How would they even know I'm a cop? Don't have a sign on my head do I? Do I have a sign on my head? Is it the moustache or what?
ANNI	They can smell it a mile off.
STEPHEN	Come on I'll be in and out.

ANNI   I said no.

                EMMA *sends a text.*

STEPHEN   I'm drunk.
                I'm wasted actually
                I've been at a wedding.
                I was best man had to give a speech.
                You get nervous you drink you know then it
                all goes pear-shaped.
                The whole thing was a fuckin' abortion if you
                wanna know the truth.
                Oh well no one remembers in the morning.
                I'm heading back there just waiting for the
                shuttle bus.
                We're going to Dick's.
                You know Dick's nightclub?

                STEPHEN *receives a text message, he reads
                it.*

                My wife.
                Something's up.
                She's pregnant.
                I'm heading out.
                Hey you should come.
                You need a break I can tell
                look at ya.
                Forget the kids call the boss tell him you're sick
                tell him you can't deal with another feral kid
                and come to Dick's with us.

ANNI   Sounds enticing.

STEPHEN   Come on.

ANNI   No.

STEPHEN   Ring the boss.

ANNI   No.

STEPHEN   Ring him here's my phone.

                EMMA *sends another text. She waits a
                moment then gathers her things to leave.*

	You don't like me do you?
ANNI	I don't have an opinion of you.
STEPHEN	Yes you have I can tell.

STEPHEN *receives the text.*

He checks it.

Wife.
You married?

ANNI	Nothing to do with you.

STEPHEN	That's a no. Boyfriend? No to that also. You're not… Oh right. Excuse me madam but I'm going to have to see your licker licence.

ANNI	Get out.

STEPHEN	Oh come on that was a joke. You're not offended are you? Are you? Are you? I'm sorry. I'm sorry Anni can I call you Anni?

ANNI	No.

STEPHEN	I love lesbians ask anyone.

ANNI	I think you should see what's wrong with your wife.

STEPHEN	It's nothing it'll be a cockroach in the room or the lamp doesn't work. It's nothing it's always nothing.

Pause.

STEPHEN	Dunno how you do it.

ANNI	What?
STEPHEN	All night cooped up in a shitty motel with a feral kid.
ANNI	It's my job.
STEPHEN	Yeah but they can be vicious little shits can't they?

Pause.

You ever been bit?

ANNI	By a dog?
STEPHEN	No by a human.
ANNI	Yeah.
STEPHEN	Me too hundreds of times. Did you know the human bite is more infectious than an animal's?
ANNI	Yes.
STEPHEN	You knew that? You're smart aren't you?

Pause.

I see you're one of them.

ANNI	One of what?
STEPHEN	A bleeding heart. You won't last long. You lot drift away too soft.
ANNI	I've been doing this job for ten years.
STEPHEN	Right that's rare.
ANNI	Is that all?
STEPHEN	Yeah that's all.
ANNI	Goodnight.
STEPHEN	Goodnight.

STEPHEN *finishes his cigarette.*

EMMA *is dressed. She's located the keys. She grabs her bag and is heading out the door when* STEPHEN *returns.*

EMMA   Who were you talking to?

STEPHEN   No one.
                Where are you going?

EMMA   I heard you talking to someone outside.

STEPHEN   What's this about?

                EMMA *is silent.*

ANNI   What happened at home Grace?
                You called me didn't you?

STEPHEN   I came back because I thought

ANNI/   something was wrong.
  STEPHEN

                EMMA *is silent.*

STEPHEN   Is there something wrong with the baby?

ANNI   Grace.

STEPHEN   What is it?
                I can't help you if you won't

ANNI/   talk to me.
  STEPHEN

ANNI   There was a dog out there.
                What happened to it?
                Do you know?

                Pause.

ANNI   Where's your mum Grace?

GRACE   Took off.
                Come home from school she's gone.
                She's always doin' that always leavin' me.
                Mum goes givin' ya up.

Givin' ya up for good this time.
Tradin' you in
want my money back.
Takin' you to Cash Converters.
Drives me to your office says I'm a this I'm a
that
see what you can do with her.
So you sit me in front of the TV put on a
DVD.
Wanna biscuit?
Wanna jelly bean?
Shove it.
You ringin' everyone beggin' 'em to take me
just for one night.
She's ADHD PTSD ODD OTT.
It's dark you still can't find anyone.
Want to go home don't you?
So you dump me at the Res.
Next day next week next month Mum's back.
Wants me misses me.
And you give me back
give me back cos I'm crap.

ANNI   Look I know that it must seem like everyone
              in your life

GRACE   I know that it must seem like everyone in
              your life

ANNI   abandons you.

GRACE   abandons you.

ANNI   I know you're angry.

GRACE   I know you're angry.

ANNI   Don't copy me please.

GRACE   Don't copy me please.

ANNI   Grace.

GRACE   Grace.

ANNI   I'm trying to talk to you.

GRACE	I'm trying to talk to you.
ANNI	Okay.
GRACE	Okay.
ANNI	Fine.
GRACE	Fine.

Long silence.

STEPHEN	What is wrong with you?
EMMA	I can't sleep here.
STEPHEN	You haven't tried.
EMMA	I can't.
STEPHEN	The bus is coming in a sec.
EMMA	I feel sick.
STEPHEN	Don't be a fucken…
EMMA	What?

Pause.

STEPHEN	You've been like this all day. Didn't say a word to anyone.
EMMA	Told you I didn't want to go.
STEPHEN	It was my mate's wedding.
EMMA	Told you that this morning Told you months ago.
STEPHEN	You didn't join in the toast.
EMMA	Yeah that was a joke. You were all so wasted you could hardly speak.
STEPHEN	You didn't eat any of the food. You didn't dance. I asked you to dance. You stood against the wall.

EMMA	I couldn't.
STEPHEN	Why couldn't you?
	Silence.
	You could have pretended to have a good time. You could have faked it.
EMMA	Is that what you did?
STEPHEN	The bus'll be here in a sec.
EMMA	Then fucking go.
STEPHEN	Can't be with you when you're like this.
EMMA	Go on.
STEPHEN	I will I'm going.
	EMMA stops him.
	She takes STEPHEN's hands.
	She holds them.
	She presses his hands against her face.
EMMA	What's happened to your hands? They were so soft once. I remember thinking that when we first met. I loved your touch.
	EMMA holds STEPHEN.
	STEPHEN responds.
	They start to move towards the bed and strip.
	EMMA stops, lies still on the bed.
STEPHEN	What? What'd I do?
EMMA	You can't wait to get back.
STEPHEN	Fuck's sake.

EMMA   You'd rather be with the boys.

STEPHEN   This again?

EMMA   Go and fuck them then.
            Go on fuck off.

            EMMA lashes out at STEPHEN, throwing sheets at him.

            He restrains her and she becomes wrapped in the sheets.

STEPHEN   Stop
            Stop.

            They struggle and collapse into play.

            I'll stay.
            Okay?

            Pause.

            I'll stay until you fall asleep.

            EMMA breaks away from him.

            ANNI is reading a case file.

ANNI   It's your birthday Grace.
            It's your birthday today.
            Happy birthday.

GRACE   What'd you get me?

ANNI   I didn't know.

            STEPHEN receives a text message, he checks it.

STEPHEN   It's the boys.
            They're waiting for me.

            GRACE points to ANNI's heart pendant.

GRACE   Give me that.

ANNI   What?

GRACE   That round your neck.

ANNI	Grace it's mine.
GRACE	Can I have it?
ANNI	I'm sorry Grace it's special to me.
GRACE	Never get what I want.
ANNI	Something else?
GRACE	Sunflowers.
ANNI	All right. I'll get you some tomorrow. Promise.
GRACE	Whole lot of 'em.
ANNI	Righto.
GRACE	They're my favourite They follow the sun. I'll show you. Say you're a sunflower.
ANNI	I'm a sunflower.
GRACE	I'll be the sun.

GRACE *takes the bedside lamp and rotates across the room.*

Follow the sun.
Follow it.

GRACE *yanks the lamp from the power point.*

The room goes dark revealing for a moment an Aboriginal boy in the room. This is JOSEPH.

GRACE *grabs her dog mask and puts it on.*

EMMA *reacts.*

ANNI	Grace.
STEPHEN	Shit.
ANNI/ STEPHEN	What is it?

GRACE	Someone here.
ANNI	Just me.
GRACE	There is.
ANNI	There's no one here Grace.

ANNI *and* STEPHEN *switch the lights on.*

GRACE/EMMA	I'm going.
ANNI	Only place we're going.
GRACE	Let's go.
STEPHEN	Where?
EMMA	Home.
STEPHEN	Now?
EMMA	Yes.
STEPHEN	Too late.
ANNI	Only place we'll go is the hospital.
STEPHEN	How you getting there?
GRACE/ STEPHEN	No.
STEPHEN	Not on your own you won't.
ANNI	If you're sick Grace.
GRACE	Not sick.
STEPHEN	There'll be fuckwits out there tonight.
EMMA	All those cops? Safe as houses you said.
STEPHEN	Yeah not us.
EMMA	Then who are you talking about?
STEPHEN	No one. Forget it.
ANNI	If you're sick Grace we're going.

GRACE	Not sick.
ANNI	I'll call the hospital.
GRACE	Never said I was sick.
ANNI	If you are sick / if there's something happening.
GRACE	I'm not sick I'm not sick you're sick.
ANNI	If there's something happening in your head you should tell me Grace.
GRACE	I'm not sick.
ANNI	You sure about that?
	GRACE *nods*.
	Then take it off Grace. It's safe here.
EMMA	Hear that?
STEPHEN	It's the wind.
GRACE	Don't make me go to the hospital Anni. It's my birthday. They put me in that room. Dark in there. Stick needles in. Don't make me Anni please.
ANNI	Take it off then Grace.
GRACE	I'll be good. I promise.
ANNI	Take it off.
GRACE	Okay Anni I'll do what you say. Be your dog. Tell me anything. Tell me to sit.
ANNI	No.

GRACE	Tell me.
ANNI	No.
GRACE	Yes tell me.
ANNI	Sit.
GRACE	See. Something else. Tell me something else. Tell me something else Anni.
ANNI	Lie down.
GRACE	Something else.
ANNI	Roll over.
GRACE	See. Something else.
ANNI	That's enough.
GRACE	Don't have to call the hospital.

GRACE *takes off the mask*.

	Don't. Staying with you aren't I Anni?
ANNI	Go to sleep.
ANNI/ STEPHEN	Try to sleep hey.

EMMA *doesn't move*.

STEPHEN	Not going to fall asleep if you don't lie down.
ANNI/ STEPHEN	Close your eyes.
EMMA	I told you.
GRACE/EMMA	I can't sleep here.
ANNI/ STEPHEN	Try.

GRACE/EMMA Can't.

ANNI You're safe.
This is a safe place.
The door is locked.

CRAIG enters the motel room in police uniform.

He carries a duffel bag.

He is agitated.

He closes the door and locks it.

He looks out at the car park through the peephole.

He throws his keys and mobile on the bed, checks out the room.

Suddenly he feels his stomach give way.

He rushes to the bathroom.

He throws up.

He flushes the toilet.

He washes his face and looks in the mirror.

He emerges from the bathroom and takes a bottle of Jim Beam from his duffel bag.

He finds a glass pours himself a drink and skulls it.

He pours another.

He sits on the bed and stares at the door.

STEPHEN Fuck it.
Let's do it.
Let's bite the bullet.
Let's get the plasma.
Let's get the fifty-two fucking inches of high definition.
That'll cheer you up.
I mean why wait?

We got the money sitting in the home deposit account.
I'll call around get the best deal.
They'll deliver it by midweek.
Fuck it.

Silence.

ANNI/ STEPHEN	Try to sleep.

EMMA   What are we doing here?

STEPHEN   We agreed to stay the night instead of driving home.
We figured I'd be pissed you'd be tired.
That's what we said.
It's a shitbox I know I'm sorry but it's all I could get.

EMMA   No why are we here in the Territory?

STEPHEN   You know why.

EMMA   You tell me.
I want you to remember what you did.

STEPHEN   Would you just go to sleep?

EMMA   If I could I fucking would.

STEPHEN   Be quiet and you might.

EMMA   You did the right thing back then.

STEPHEN   Did I?

EMMA   Yes you did.

STEPHEN   Where'd it get me?
Posted to this shithole.

EMMA   I was proud of you then.

STEPHEN   We'd be living it up on the Gold Coast
by now if I'd just shut my mouth.

EMMA   It's happened again.

STEPHEN	No it hasn't.
EMMA	No you're right. This time is different.
STEPHEN	You were the one who said let's make a go of it. Do something useful out here. You said that.
EMMA	I thought we could. I was wrong.
STEPHEN	So you just packed it in. Quit teaching. You didn't really try.
EMMA	I tried. I fucking tried. I couldn't do it any more.
STEPHEN	Why not?
EMMA	I couldn't help those kids. I didn't even know where to begin.
STEPHEN	One plus one? There's a start.
EMMA	You wouldn't understand.
STEPHEN	Yeah I'm a dumb cop. That's what you think isn't it? At least I'm out there every day. DVOs stabbings shootings ODs rapes. Fuckin' smorgasbord of horror. What if we all just left? Packed it in pissed off? Place'd go to the fuckin' dogs. You know it.
EMMA	He hardly ever came to school that boy.

Who could blame him?
One day he turned up
for breakfast probably.
Some kids came up
tell me he's in the girls' toilets.
hiding in one of the cubicles
crying.
So I went in there.
He was singing this weird song
Eeny meeny miny mo catch a...
I told him you have a beautiful voice.
It was beautiful but it scared me.
I asked him to come out of there but he
wouldn't.
He was so distressed.
He yelled at me.
Fuck off white cunt.
I had to call for help.
I didn't hear about him again until...
I couldn't get his voice out of my head.
Fuck
off
white
cunt.
So I did.
I couldn't help him.

Pause.

We should never have come here.
Everything's been fucked since we came here.

STEPHEN	That's not true.
EMMA	Yes.
STEPHEN	What about the baby?

Silence.

EMMA	I want to go home. Let's go home to Sydney.
STEPHEN	Yeah then what would I do?

EMMA   Anything but this.

STEPHEN   It's my job.
                It's who I am.

EMMA   And who's that?

                Pause

STEPHEN   I've missed the bus now.
                Where are the keys?

EMMA   Don't go back.

STEPHEN   I told Craig I would.

EMMA   You're scared of him.
                That's it.

                STEPHEN *scoffs*.

                You are.
                You're scared of the top dog.
                I was watching you today
                at the reception.
                I was watching you with him
                with the whole pack.
                He's really got you all to heel.
                How does he do that?
                How does he get such loyalty?
                That's what I want to know.

STEPHEN   Least the force is loyal Emma.
                Always has been.

EMMA   Yeah?
                Well I could've disappeared for hours
                you wouldn't have even known.

STEPHEN   Bullshit.

EMMA   You don't have to go.

STEPHEN   I wanna go out.
                I wanna get blotto.
                We'll talk about this tomorrow.

EMMA   What if I'm not here?

GRACE	You got a baby?
EMMA	What if I'm gone?
	EMMA *picks up her bag, goes to the bathroom and locks the door.*
	Pause.
ANNI	No.
GRACE	Too old?
ANNI	Too tired maybe late nights like this.
GRACE	You hate kids.
ANNI	Why would I work with kids if I hated them?
GRACE	You're a paedo. Paedos get jobs with kids so they can rape 'em.
ANNI	I like kids when they're not biting me.
GRACE	You hate me.
ANNI	That's not true.
GRACE	Do you like me?
ANNI	Yeah I do.
	Pause.
GRACE	Do you love me? You bought me a Heart.
ANNI	Yes I did.
GRACE	I'm havin' a baby. Soon as I can I will soon as possible. Held one once.
ANNI	Did you?
GRACE	Once I did.
ANNI	Did you like that?
GRACE	Yes.

There's a place at the front of their head that's
soft.
Can't press it hard or you kill them
did you know that?

ANNI   Yes.

GRACE   Pressed it gentle.

ANNI   That's good.

GRACE   I took its clothes off
           stuck my finger in its mouth.
           Then I licked it.

ANNI   Whose baby was it?

GRACE   It cried.

ANNI   Whose baby was it Grace?

GRACE   Don't remember now.
           Know what an abortion is?

ANNI   Yeah.

GRACE   Know what they do?

ANNI   I got a fair idea.

GRACE   They cut 'em up inside you
           then pull 'em out your gash bit by bit.

ANNI   It's not like that.

GRACE   Arms 'n' legs 'n' head 'n' heart.

ANNI   Who told you that?

GRACE   Mum.
           She says she should've done that.
           Says I got bad in me.
           I have haven't I Anni?

ANNI   No.

GRACE   It's inside me.

ANNI   No.

GRACE   Yes.

ANNI   That's not true.

GRACE   Yes.
             You'll see.

STEPHEN   Fuck this I'm going.
             Said I'm going back.

             *STEPHEN searches the room for the car
             keys.*

             Where are the keys?
             Where'd you put the keys Em?

             He can't locate them.

             He stands at the bathroom door.

             Hey?
             Do you have the keys?

             *EMMA shakes the car keys from inside the
             bathroom.*

             Pause.

             Open the door Emma.
             Can you open the door for a tick?

             Pause.

             They'll be wondering where I am.
             Can you open the fucking door?

             Pause.

             You want me to ram it down?
             I can do that.
             I've done that before.
             I can do that.

             Silence.

             Please open the door.
             Open it.

             STEPHEN bangs on the door.

CRAIG *inspects the contents of a McDonald's bag.*

He turns and addresses STEPHEN.

CRAIG   You took your time.

STEPHEN   Yeah I was...

CRAIG   All these motels look the fuckin' same hey?

STEPHEN   Yeah.

CRAIG   Sit down.

STEPHEN   I gotta get back.
              I'm on in an hour.

CRAIG   Sit down have a drink.

STEPHEN   I said I'd be / back.

CRAIG   Sit.

              CRAIG *pours* STEPHEN *a drink.*

              Feel like the fuckin' fugitive mate.
              Harrison fucking Ford.

              Silence.

              So who have we got coming from Darwin?

STEPHEN   Inspector Johnson.

CRAIG   Johno?
              Good one.
              Who else?

STEPHEN   Derwent

CRAIG   Great.

STEPHEN   and Grant.

CRAIG   Who's he when he's at home?

STEPHEN   He'll be a junior on the investigation.

CRAIG   Some shit-kicker.
              When do they get here?

STEPHEN	I'm picking them up from the airstrip tonight.
CRAIG	What time?
STEPHEN	Eight-thirty.
CRAIG	Tell you what swing by.
STEPHEN	Hey?
CRAIG	Pick 'em up swing by here. We'll have a drink. Johno and me go way back we're old mates. It's on your way. And bring us another bottle of Jim when you come.
STEPHEN	Yeah righto.
CRAIG	When are they flying me out?
STEPHEN	Soon as they do the interview I guess.
CRAIG	When's that scheduled?
STEPHEN	First thing tomorrow.

Pause.

CRAIG	Family been informed?
STEPHEN	Just then just now.
CRAIG	You?

STEPHEN *nods.*

I'm going to recommend they bring a squad
in from Darwin.

STEPHEN	You think that's necessary?
CRAIG	With just the three of youse yes I think it's fuckin' necessary. Once something like this gets wind.

How's the station going to hold up?
My house.
That'll be the first place they target.
Fuckin' bike gym stereo.
Say goodbye to all that.

STEPHEN   Maybe we should just wait for the coronial.
               Shit'll probably settle in a few days.

CRAIG   That what you reckon?
               Don't underestimate this place.
               This place is like a fuckin' scab.
               You just gotta pick it and it starts pissing
               blood
               pissing rage.

               Silence.

               How's Emma?

STEPHEN   Yeah good.

CRAIG   Not what I heard.

STEPHEN   Why what'd you hear?

CRAIG   Heard she's a bit unhappy.

STEPHEN   She's all right.

CRAIG   Quit her job at the school.

STEPHEN   We're having a baby.

CRAIG   It's tough in the Territory
               no question.
               You can't be soft.
               Like my old man says
               sometimes you have to drink a glass of
               cement and harden the fuck up.
               Blame you does she?

STEPHEN   Why would she?

CRAIG   You tell me.

               Pause.

STEPHEN	It's the job. She knows that. We go where I'm sent. Make the most of it.
CRAIG	Any time you need anything you just have to ask.
STEPHEN	Thanks.

STEPHEN *goes to leave but* CRAIG *blocks his way and refills his glass.*

CRAIG	You saw him fall didn't you? In his intoxicated state he tripped.
STEPHEN	I was on the desk.
CRAIG	That's right and from that angle you saw…
STEPHEN	I didn't see anything.
CRAIG	From that angle you saw that we had a little scuffle on our way in. He fell.

STEPHEN *is silent.*

Do you have a problem Constable?

STEPHEN	Just the OPM…
CRAIG	'Members directly involved in the incident should not discuss the incident amongst themselves prior to being interviewed.' Right?
STEPHEN	Yeah.
CRAIG	Fuck the OPM. Written by lawyer cunts with no fuckin' idea of the reality. Right? And he was mouthing off wasn't he? You would've heard all that?
STEPHEN	Yeah he called you a queenie cunt.

CRAIG   No.

STEPHEN   He didn't call you a queenie cunt?

CRAIG   He was the one wearing the fuckin' dress
off his fucking face in the middle of the street
causing a disturbance.
Fuckin' Mardi Gras parade.

Pause.

So he's mouthing off and I said to him.
Do you have a problem with police?
And he bit me.
The vicious little shit fuckin' bit me.
We had a scuffle
he fell and I put him in the cell to sleep it off.

Silence.

I then inserted a tape into the surveillance
monitor
and attended to my paperwork.
That's where you come in Constable.

STEPHEN   What?

CRAIG   Wha?
Half an hour later you went to check on him.
Is that correct?

STEPHEN   Yeah I went to check on him.
He was unconscious on the floor of the cell.
I kicked him.

CRAIG   You used an arousal technique.

STEPHEN   I used an arousal technique.
I checked his pulse
couldn't find one
then I called the ambulance.

Pause.

CRAIG   How long have we known each other Collins?

STEPHEN   Three years.

CRAIG   Three years that's right.
                 What do you know about me?
                 Come on.
                 What have you heard?
                 Be honest.

STEPHEN   I don't know.
                 Your dad was a cop.
                 Your dad's dad was a cop.

CRAIG   Yeah yeah apart from that.

STEPHEN   You can drink a bottle of Jim
                 and still shoot a target at one hundred metres.

CRAIG   That is fuckin' true.
                 What else?

STEPHEN   You've been here eight years.

CRAIG   That's right.
                 Eight years and I've worked my arse off to
                 earn the respect of this community.
                 What else?

STEPHEN   Done a lot for the local kids.

CRAIG   The sports trips right.
                 I'm like a dad to a lot of these kids.
                 I didn't say that someone else said that.
                 That was a quote in the paper.
                 Anything else?
                 Got anything else on me?

STEPHEN   No.

CRAIG   No?
                 You sure about that?
                 Now's your chance to have a go.
                 Go on.
                 Free hit.

                 Pause.

                 One thing you should know about this town.
                 Every arsehole knows your business

and if they don't they make the shit up.
Some cunts wanna see a good man go down.

STEPHEN   I better head.

CRAIG   Tell you something I heard about you mate.

Pause

Heard a rumour you were a squealer.
Heard you squealed like a little pig.
But I reckon that's bullshit.
Like I said some cunts wanna see a good man
go down.

STEPHEN *heads to the door.*

Stephen?
Guess what?
I'm getting hitched.
Been thinking I might as well tie the knot.
Good a time as any.
What do you reckon?

STEPHEN   Yeah good one congratulations.

GRACE *is chanting 'Eeny, Meeny, Miny, Mo'
silently.*

We see a glimpse of JOSEPH *in the wardrobe
playing the game with* GRACE.

JOSEPH *disappears.*

ANNI   Grace look at me.
Look at me Grace.

GRACE   Eeny meeny miny mo
catch a faggot by the toe
if he squeals cut his prick off
eeny meeny miny mo.
That means you're a faggot.

Pause.

Eeny meeny miny mo
catch a faggot by the toe

	if he squeals cut his prick off eeny meeny miny mo. That means I'm a faggot.
ANNI	Who taught you that?
GRACE	A faggot. Do you like it?
ANNI	No.
GRACE	Why not? Why not?

GRACE *continues chanting 'Eeny, Meeny, Miny, Mo'.*

ANNI *watches her.*

CRAIG *is drinking.*

The sound of rocks hitting the windows and door of the motel.

CRAIG *hears this and is suddenly alert.*

He goes to the peephole in the door and looks out.

He sees no one.

He opens the door and scans the car park.

There's no one out there.

EMMA *emerges from the bathroom.*

She throws the keys on the bed.

CRAIG *goes to the bathroom.*

STEPHEN *collects the keys.*

STEPHEN	You need help. You're fucked up. Psycho.
EMMA	You make me that way.
STEPHEN	You embarrassed me at the wedding.

EMMA   Did I?

STEPHEN   Yes.

EMMA   I embarrassed you in front of the boys did I?

STEPHEN   What's wrong with Emma
              they were asking me?
              Doesn't she like us?
              I told 'em you were just tired that's all.
              I know they're all thinking you're a stuck-up
              bitch.
              I'm always defending you.

              Pause.

EMMA   He cornered me today.

STEPHEN   Who?

EMMA   The groom.
              Craig.
              Your best mate.
              He cornered me on my way to the bathroom.

              CRAIG *emerges from the bathroom.*

              An image of EMMA *and* CRAIG *in close
              proximity.*

              He pushed me against the wall.
              He stunk.
              I could feel his dick on my leg.
              He wanted to know if I 'blessed his union'
              said it like that.
              So I said
              You're fucked anyway Craig.
              I'd fuck off out of here if I were you.
              Everyone knows what you did.

              EMMA *laughs.*

STEPHEN   Fuck
              why'd you say that?

EMMA   He looked like he wanted to hit me.

STEPHEN	Fuck.
EMMA	He wanted to shut me up with this fist. He looked scared.
	CRAIG *moves away.*
STEPHEN	You are fucking kidding me.
EMMA	You've told him what I said haven't you?
STEPHEN	I don't believe this shit.
EMMA	You told him I think he bashed that boy
STEPHEN	Why would I tell him that?
EMMA	bashed him so bad he bled to death.
STEPHEN	He fell down the fuckin' stairs.
EMMA	Not by accident.
STEPHEN	The inquest is over. Fucking forget it.
EMMA	He was a kid throwing rocks at a street sign.
STEPHEN	He was off his face. He was a danger to himself.
EMMA	And now the boy is dead.
STEPHEN	You weren't there.
EMMA	You didn't hear him calling for help? It was on the surveillance tape. He was calling for help for half an hour. You didn't hear that?
STEPHEN	I'm not going to be cross-examined by my own fucking wife on my mate's wedding night.
	Pause.
EMMA	It wasn't a wedding it was a rally a fuck-you to this community. We got away with it. We'll always get away with it. Now we're all fucked because of him.

STEPHEN	He can't fuckin' win.
EMMA	Why are you protecting him?
STEPHEN	It's this town. Every arsehole knows your business and if they don't they make the shit up. Some cunts just wanna bring a good man down.

EMMA stares at STEPHEN.

EMMA	You're all dogs.

STEPHEN charges at EMMA and nearly hits her.

She flinches.

He hits the door instead.

Go on you can do that.
You've done it before.

Silence.

STEPHEN	Do not call me that. I get called that by maggots then I come home and my own

Pause.

wife calls me that.

STEPHEN leaves the room.

GRACE suddenly goes to her backpack.

ANNI	What are you doing Grace?

She buries her hand in the bag and pulls out something bloodied and wrapped in a shirt.

GRACE places it on the bed.

She turns to ANNI.

ANNI	What's that?
GRACE	It's for you.

ANNI	What is it?
GRACE	Something from home. Something special.
ANNI	What is it Grace?
GRACE	Open it.
	ANNI *approaches the object cautiously.*
	She unwraps it to reveal a bloodied heart.
	ANNI *recoils.*
	It's a heart. It's for you.
ANNI	Where'd you get this? Where did you get this Grace?
GRACE	The dog.
ANNI	What dog?
GRACE	Dog you saw.
ANNI	The dog at your place? Did you do that? Did you kill that dog Grace?
GRACE	He was my favourite. Smashed his brain with a hammer. Cut this out. Cut it with a knife. It's a heart. It's for you.
ANNI	Get rid of it.
GRACE	Barking too much. Never shut up. Don't you like it?
ANNI	Said get rid of it.
GRACE	It's for you.
ANNI	I don't want it.

GRACE   But it's for you.

ANNI   I don't want it Grace.

GRACE   Why not?
         Why not?

         ANNI *wraps up the heart and puts it in the bin. She ties the garbage bag and takes the bin into the bathroom.*

         GRACE *is staring at* ANNI *when she emerges.*

         Do you hate me Anni?
         You scared of me yet?

         EMMA *pulls herself together, finds the Jim Beam bottle and pours herself a glass.*

         She drinks.

         The sound of rocks on the window of the motel.

         EMMA *chants 'Eeny, Meeny, Miny, Mo'.*

         GRACE *hears the sound also.*

         He's coming.

ANNI   Who's coming?

         CRAIG *rushes to the door. He opens it.*

CRAIG   Piss off.

         He steps outside, looks around, there's no one.

         He goes back inside and locks the door.

ANNI   Where's your mum Grace?
         I thought I saw her out there up at the shed.
         The police are there now.
         What happened?
         Who were you hiding from under the house?

         GRACE *grabs her bag and makes a circle of dirt around the bed.*

ANNI/ STEPHEN	What are you doing?
GRACE	Makin' a trap.
ANNI	For what?
GRACE	So we'll see his footprints.
ANNI	No.
ANNI/ STEPHEN	Stop.
ANNI	You can't spread dirt around a motel room.
ANNI/ STEPHEN	Stop.
ANNI	You can't do that.
GRACE	Keepin' us safe.
ANNI	No more. Stop that's enough.
GRACE	Go to bed now Anni.
ANNI	Okay I'll do what you say but I need you to tell me what's happened.
GRACE	Yes go to sleep.
ANNI	I'm not going to sleep.
GRACE	It's all right you can. I'll keep watch.
	GRACE *is manic, agitated.*
	STEPHEN *watches* EMMA *finish the drink.*
	She pours another.
STEPHEN	Will you please stop?
	EMMA *drinks in silence.*
	Please? Are you trying to punish me?

ANNI *watches* GRACE.

ANNI	What's happening in your head? Hey?
GRACE	Nothing.
ANNI	Talk to me please.
GRACE	Nothing I said.
ANNI	Please Grace.

GRACE *stalks* ANNI.

GRACE	Can smell you. I'm like a dog. Can smell your blood. Smell your bleeding.
ANNI	Back off. Back off Grace. I said back off. I won't say it again.
GRACE	Just trying to talk to ya bitch.
ANNI	And I'm trying to help you Grace.
GRACE	Too late. I'm already fucked.
EMMA	Don't you like this?
STEPHEN	No.
EMMA	Why not?
STEPHEN	Our child…
EMMA	So what? Children die all the time every day. One less so fucking what?
STEPHEN	You don't mean that.

Pause.

GRACE	Gotta go. Gotta go now. Let's go.
ANNI	What's happening?
GRACE	Take me home with you.
ANNI	I can't do that.
GRACE	Why not?
ANNI	It's against the rules you know that. I wish I could.
GRACE	Please Anni please Anni please Anni please. Wanna be with you. Wanna be with you You promised me you promised me. Take me home with you now. Please. Please Anni.

GRACE *is crying.*

ANNI	Hey it's okay Grace. Calm down.
GRACE	He's coming soon. He's coming here.
ANNI	Who? Look at me. Look at me Grace. Hey. It's okay.

ANNI *holds* GRACE.

EMMA *puts her drinks down.*

EMMA	Do you know when I found out I was pregnant in Sydney I saw a doctor. I told her I wanted it gone out of me.

Couldn't bear the thought of bringing it into
this.
I was sitting in the car outside the clinic.
I'd just lit a cigarette
and you called.

Pause.

I would have gone through with it.

STEPHEN   Why'd you come back?

EMMA   I don't know.
You sounded so happy when I told you.
I'd forgotten you had a heart.

ANNI *takes off her heart pendant.*

ANNI   Here.
It's yours.

GRACE   It's a heart.

STEPHEN   I love you so much.

ANNI   It's for you.

GRACE   It's forever.

EMMA   You lied to me.
You lied to me and you keep lying and lying.
And I'm terrified that one day I'll wake up
and I won't know you at all.
Stephen?
Stephen?

I shouldn't have answered your call.

ANNI   Happy birthday Grace.

GRACE *hits* ANNI *and knocks her out cold.*

GRACE   See
I told you cunt.

EMMA *rushes to the bathroom to throw up.*

STEPHEN *goes out for a smoke.*

The lights flicker.

He's here.

CRAIG *stands and approaches the wardrobe.*

He opens the door of the wardrobe to reveal
JOSEPH *wearing a wedding dress and*
holding a dog's heart.

JOSEPH *is badly bruised.*

JOSEPH   Boo.

CRAIG   You the one throwing rocks?
           Out here
           in the light.

           JOSEPH *steps out and walks towards the*
           light.

           Who did that?

JOSEPH   Don't you know me?

CRAIG   What do you want?

JOSEPH   Want to be with you.

CRAIG   No.

JOSEPH   I'm lonely.
           I'm scared of the dark.
           Hear them?
           They howl all night.
           Want to be with you.

           CRAIG *shakes his head.*

           You owe me.

           Pause.

           Remember this dress?

           CRAIG *shakes his head.*

           Yes.
           Bought it at the Salvos.
           I'm wearin' it in the street.

Got a bag of rocks.
I'm throwin' 'em at street signs.
Just for fun.
Not hurting anyone.
That's when you come.
I know you.
You're that big cop.
Take kids to the city on footy trips.
Take me?

CRAIG   Not you.

JOSEPH   How come?

CRAIG   Something wrong with you.

JOSEPH   Same as you.
            Know what you are.

CRAIG   What am I?

JOSEPH   Don't you like me?
            You say.

CRAIG   Put down the rock.

            JOSEPH *doesn't move*.

            Put the rock
            on the ground
            now.
            What's your name?

            JOSEPH *is silent*.

            Do you want to come for a ride down the
            station?

            JOSEPH *dances*.

JOSEPH   Do you think I'm a good dancer?
            Dance with me.
            Hold me.
            Please.
            I'm lonely.
            Please.

CRAIG *moves towards* JOSEPH, *they hold each other and dance for some time.*

CRAIG *cries then breaks away from* JOSEPH.

JOSEPH *whispers in* CRAIG*'s ear.*

Queenie cunt.

CRAIG *rips away from* JOSEPH.

CRAIG   What did you say?

JOSEPH   Eeny
meeny
miny
mo.

CRAIG   What did you say to me?

JOSEPH   Catch
a
faggot
by
the
toe.

CRAIG   Why are you here?

JOSEPH   If
he
squeals
let
him
go.
Eeny
meeny
miny

Pause.

Mo.
I'm waiting for you.

CRAIG *goes for* JOSEPH.

JOSEPH *morphs into a dog and attacks*
CRAIG *on the bed.*

I fuck your head.
I fuck your prick.
I fuck your heart.

Darkness.

JOSEPH *recedes into darkness.*

CRAIG *is alone clutching his chest.*

Darkness.

Light.

CRAIG *is gone.*

STEPHEN *approaches* EMMA. *He touches*
EMMA's *stomach.*

EMMA *turns away from him and leaves.*

Darkness.

Light.

GRACE *is staring at the mirror.*

She is wearing the dog mask.

Darkness.

Light.

GRACE *stares at the motel door.*

Darkness.

Light.

GRACE *is sitting on the bed holding the
knife.*

Darkness.

Light.

ANNI   Grace.

GRACE	You're calling them now. Aren't you Anni? You're gunna call the hospital now.
	GRACE *lifts the knife to stab herself.*
ANNI	No.
	Darkness.
	ANNI *sits at the foot of the bed holding a sunflower.*
STEPHEN	You're alone here. There's no client arriving tonight is there?
	Pause.
ANNI	No.
STEPHEN	It was this room wasn't it? I was involved in that case. The girl.
ANNI	Grace.
STEPHEN	Hey?
ANNI	Her name was Grace.
STEPHEN	Bad shit happens. Happens all the time. Gotta let it go. Nothing you can do.
ANNI	Easy for you.
STEPHEN	How you figure that?
ANNI	Charge in shove people around lock 'em up beat 'em up.
STEPHEN	Hey?
ANNI	One less vicious shit one less maggot. Job done. Knock off have a laugh have a beer with your mates.

Don't have to try and fix anything
put together the pieces of some poor kid's
fucked-up life.
Don't have to feel don't have to think.

Silence.

Perhaps STEPHEN *puts out his cigarette and goes to leave.*

He stops.

STEPHEN   What are you doing here?

ANNI   It's my birthday.
I was having dinner at home with my family.
All the people I love.
But I had to leave the table because
all I could think of was her
her in this dark place.

Pause.

STEPHEN   I was called out there.

ANNI   Yeah I know.

STEPHEN   You read the police report?

ANNI   Yeah.

STEPHEN   Yeah.

Pause.

ANNI   Tell me.
Go on.
Tell me what happened.

STEPHEN   No.

ANNI   Why?

STEPHEN   I want to forget it.

ANNI   But you can't can you?
Tell me what you saw out there
what Grace saw.

STEPHEN   I went out there alone
                 no back-up.
                 We were a man down
                 stretched to the limits.
                 It was dark when I got there.
                 Dogs going mad.
                 Dead one out the front
                 crawling with flies.
                 It'd been axed in the leg
                 dragging itself around who knows how long.
                 Looked like someone had smashed its head
                 with a brick.

ANNI   Grace.
                 She didn't kill it.
                 She put it down.

STEPHEN   Dark inside the house.
                 I pulled my weapon.
                 Power was cut.
                 There was this bad smell.
                 Flies food shit.
                 I called out.
                 Police.
                 Is there anyone here?
                 Nothing.
                 House was empty.
                 I go up the hill to the shed.
                 Doors are wide open.
                 See a man hanging from one of the steel
                 beams.
                 No sign of the woman yet.
                 I go round the back.
                 There's a sedan.
                 The boot packed
                 tied down with rope.
                 Go round the side.
                 She's in the driver's seat.
                 Blood everywhere.
                 She was trying to leave
                 and he axed her to death.

Her hair
the woman's hair was covering her face.
So I reached my hand through the car window
to brush it away.
Then I made the call for back-up.
I waited with her in the dark till they came.

STEPHEN *cries*.

ANNI   You and your wife should leave here.
Get out before it's too late
Never should have come here in the first
place.

STEPHEN *disappears into darkness,*

ANNI *continues as if he's still there*.

I saw her out there.
Grace's mother.
She was up by the shed.
She was waving at me.

Pause.

Maybe she didn't know she was dead.

Darkness.

End of Play.

A Nick Hern Book

The Dark Room first published in Great Britain in 2017 as a paperback original by Nick Hern Books Limited, The Glasshouse, 49a Goldhawk Road, London W12 8QP, by arrangement with Playlab, PO Box 3701, South Brisbane BC, Queensland, Australia, www.playlab.org.au

First published by Playlab in 2009

Cover photograph © iStockPhoto.com/jodie777

Designed and typeset by Nick Hern Books, London
Printed in Great Britain by Mimeo Ltd, Huntingdon, Cambridgeshire PE29 6XX

A CIP catalogue record for this book is available from the British Library

ISBN 978 1 84842 727 3